The tales of trials and triumph

Sudi A. Mohamud

The Tales of Trials and Triumph

Published by BooxAi

ISBN: 978-965-578-809-9

The tales of trials and triumph

MY AUTOBIOGRAPHY

SUDI A. MOHAMUD

Contents

I would love to take a moment to thank my family and friends who helped me with this book. I am sincerely grateful.

Yasin Cisse
Advisor/Partner
Amal Adan
Supporter/Advisor
Ahmed Ibrahim
Marketing/Technology Consultant
Adem Shimbirolays
Poet, author, composer, historian, musician and social justice activist

Chapter One

My name is Sucdi Abdi Mohamud, and this is my story. I was born in Mogadishu, the capital of Somalia, in 1982 —when the eighties were vibrant and full of hope. As the youngest child in a family of twelve, which consisted of three brothers and eight sisters, I always looked up to my older siblings. They guided me on the right path and instilled essential values I still hold dear.

My mother was born in **Bardele**, Gedo, and my father was born in Galmudug, Somalia.

My mother spent half of her life in Gedo. She held a unique position as the oldest sibling among her mother's children while also being the youngest sibling in her father's family. Her father had two spouses. This duality profoundly shaped her perspective and contributed to the richness of her experience. In the Islamic religion, a man can take up to four wives if he has the means to support them and if it aligns with their religious and cultural tradition. This can have various social, economic, and religious implications, and it is deeply rooted in the history and traditions of the communities. My grandmother belonged to a royal tribe. My mother and her siblings grew up with all the resources they needed available to them, but that changed when my grandmother died. Although my mother oversaw everything, the farm, the animals, and the stuff, in our culture, if you do not have a man in your life, you are considered unlucky or unwanted, so it's preferred you marry so that the husband can help with raising the children and look after the family.

In my mother's situation, she married when she was sixteen. She had her first child when she was seventeen and her second when she was nineteen, but her husband grew insecure in their marriage. He became power-hungry, seizing control of all my mother's family possessed after her father died, and began beating my mother and the staff.

As a result, my mother left the marriage as soon as she could, taking her two children and moving to Galmudug, Somalia. She was certain that she could provide a better life for herself and her children.

My father was born in Galmudug, Somalia, as the third of five children. My father used to look after the animals on his father's farm. His father was considered wealthy in Somalia, and my father had the most significant resources accessible to him.

Growing up in that environment, his extended uncle

on his mother's side gifted him a girl when he was twenty and she was eighteen. In Somalia, you were considered important to someone if they gifted you a girl. They had an intimate wedding with their family and friends from the village. They slaughtered ten of their camels and donated the meat to the poor. The bride wore a traditional Somali dress, and her hair was braided. As a dowry, he gifted the bride's family with camels. A few months later, the couple were blessed to be welcoming twins. His new bride had a safe pregnancy, and everything was going well until the night she was in labor. Due to a lack of medical resources and the presence of a medical professional, she ended up having major complications and succumbed to her death. The children were raised by their grandmother. A few years later, my father went into the city to buy sugar, and while he was walking down the street, he saw my mother sitting under a tree sewing a blanket; she was wearing a red dress. He asked her where the market was, and she gave him the directions. He came back an hour later, and she was still sewing. He decided to talk to her because he knew she was new to town. They talked for a bit. He went to his mother's, and his mother asked him why he was late; he responded by telling her about the woman he had met and how she knew how to sew and was good with her hands. His mother said, "If she knows how to sew clothes, then we'll go to her and exchange milk for some clothing." The day after, they met her and exchanged two gallons of milk for some clothes. Since my mother always sat in the same spot, it was easy to find her. After they found her, his mother asked how long it would take her to sew clothes for six people. My mother replied, "If I have the materials, it will only take me a day." His Mother was impressed. His mother asked, "Where is your family." My mother responded with, "I'm from Gedo." "Why are you all the way here?" His mother asked. "I came to visit my cousins," My mother replied. "Who are your cousins?" His mother asked. After my mother told her who her cousins were, his mother told her that she knew the family, gave her some milk, and said she would be there before sundown tomorrow to pick up the clothes. My mother asked, "I have not measured anyone; how can you pick up the clothes? My grandma told her, "Start with me and my son, then I will bring my husband tomorrow." My mom asked her what her favorite color was so she could get the materials. My grandmother answered, "My favorite colors are blue, red, and white."

She did not know that my grandmother was checking to see if she was a good fit for her son. My grandmother became so excited since she knew my mom's family very well. They talked about my mom and how she was a good fit for my dad.

When they reached the house, my grandpa asked, "What are you two happy about?" But before they answered, the little boy said, "Grandma found a lady for my dad." Confused, my grandpa said, "What do you mean?" Grandma said, "Your best friend has a cousin who came from Gedo, and I want her to be my daughter-in-law so she can take care of the twins." Then my grandpa answered, "I know the family, and I know the lady you are referring to, but did you know she is divorced and that she comes from a royal family?" My grandma asked, "Really?" "Yes," my grandpa said. My dad, confused, said, "Royal or not, I want that lady. She's very nice and kind". On the other side, my mom was attracted to how handsome he was, and she asked her cousin about my dad and his family. The next day, my grandpa and grandma came to see my mom. She had already made two items of clothes. My grandpa said, "We have not met; how do you know my size? My mom said, "I just guested." He was so impressed.

That day before the sundown, my grandpa went to see her cousin to ask for her hand in marriage. In Somali culture, it is very respectful to go to the hierarchy, and since it was love at first sight, they were both happy. They had their wedding a week later, just like the last time they sacrificed an animal. They danced together with their four children, and they wore the clothes my mom had made for the wedding.

Two weeks later, they decided to move to Mogadishu, the Capital of Somalia, to give their children a better education and more opportunities. My dad found a job right away so he could support his new family, and my mom was always good at sewing. They both worked until my mom became pregnant. It was their first child, and my dad was so excited that he told my mom to stay home, and he made sure she had housekeeping help around the house. They lived a happy life with their children.

Years later, the twins were grown-ups and started working part-time. My mother was raising ten children. We had a big house, garden security, and a guard. Life was great, and they were happy together; they believed they could conquer everything and anything that came their way. Mom taught her children how to sew. My sister was so good at sewing. She decided to open a store next to the house and help mom raise the kids. My half-brother joined the army, but he was able to come home every night.

Besides all the help, money was becoming tight, so mom decided to apply to prestigious boarding schools. It usually took a year or two, but in that case, four years passed while my mother awaited an answer. From school, mom dreamed about being pregnant and sitting in the front of the house. Nine months later, I came along. When mom found out she was pregnant, everybody was expecting a boy, but when I was born, and mom found out that I was a girl, she was over the moon. The day I was born was rainy and cold, which was rare; everybody was wondering what was going on. And that's how I came along in this beautiful world: I was 6 lbs. 4 oz. My dad was so excited that he had a daughter because he always said daughters were blessed by God. He came up with the name Sudi, but my mom and everyone else, including my sister, had their own ideas. Everyone called me a name of their own. I was the luckiest girl on earth. I had a lot of sisters and brothers who could take care of me regardless of where life took us. I used to enjoy my brother and my sisters. I chose to keep the name my father bestowed upon me but kept my other names close to my heart. I was the queen of the house until the day my dad lost his job because the economy changed. So, our neighbors and our Somali community became our extended family, providing comfort during troubled times for our family.

Growing up, I dreamed of becoming a social worker, hoping to make a positive difference in people's lives. By leaning on my internal value system, I aimed to build bridges instead of burning them down, as was the political climate at the time. However, those dreams faded away as our city was torn apart by civil war. Tribal infighting had become so chaotic that all meaningful communication between the people of Mogadishu completely broke down. This is when everything changed. But let us start from the beginning…

My mother sent my two older sisters and me to enroll in a prestigious boarding school at the age of three. She believed the school would provide us with educational opportunities that would open doors for us as we grew into women; she was a forward thinker. While there, people stole our clothes and food, and we were abused. My older sister used to visit every Friday and tried to make us look good in her eyes so she would not tell our

When honor and prestige become central to inter-group relations, it can exacerbate existing divisions and conflicts, leading to various negative consequences, including violence, discrimination, and social fragmentation. The pursuit of honor and prestige may lead to competition and rivalry among different groups, perpetuating a cycle of animosity and distrust.

Addressing this issue requires a multifaceted approach that involves challenging and transforming traditional norms and attitudes related to honor and prestige. Promoting alternative values such as cooperation, mutual respect, and understanding can help mitigate the negative impact of honor-based divisions.

Additionally, efforts to empower women, promote gender equality, and challenge traditional gender roles can play a crucial role in addressing honor-related conflicts, as women are often disproportionately affected by honor-based violence and restrictions.

Community-based initiatives, education, and awareness campaigns can also play a vital role in promoting dialogue, cooperation, and understanding among different groups. By fostering an environment of inclusivity and respect for diversity, it is possible to mitigate the impact of honor and prestige-driven divisions and work towards building more cohesive and harmonious societies.

Addressing tribal infighting driven by concerns over family honor and prestige requires a sustained and comprehensive effort, engaging all levels of society to foster positive change and promote a culture of peace and mutual respect.

The roads were terrifying because families were losing everything, including their children. And children were losing their parents.

Our experience was worse. My father was killed in the process of helping our families escape. Teenage girls were getting raped by the malicious warlords. These warlords kidnaped, raped, and forced adolescent girls into marriage. Now, my mother had to deal with her husband dying but also protect the rest of us, especially since there were teenage girls involved. My mother was trying to protect us, and she used to make us hide behind bushes during the day, and we traveled at night with no shoes on our feet.

So she made us travel during the night and hide, during which I never understood what was happening. The scarcity of food and unsafe water posed a threat to all Somalis. While traveling, my mom made me mess around with the footsteps we would leave behind so that the warlords would not follow them.

We were also afraid of the animals that could have killed us. We were starving, and we had to hunt animals to survive. Most of us became sick after a while. After 15 days, we finally reached Berdaale, a small city in Gedo. After arriving at my mom's little sister's house in Berdaale, most of the people who were sick passed out.

My aunt gave us goat and camel milk and white rice to help combat the sickness, but instead, that caused us to become even sicker. So, we decided to see a doctor, who provided us with expired medicine.

My sister took the medication the doctor had given her and became sicker than the rest of us. The rest of us took another 15 days to heal completely, but for my sister, it took her a month to heal.

My mother was more concerned about us. We thought we had found safety, but the conflict caught up in 1993, shattering our sense of security. That is when my family made the difficult choice to move to a new country, Kenya, hoping for a life free from the violence that haunted us. However, at the same time, the thought of leaving everything we knew behind was too unbearable to contemplate. Where would we go? Who would help us? Could we speak the language? Where would we live? These thoughts ran through the minds of everyone living in Somalia. We were now officially nomads in the literal sense, not just in spirit—displaced people in Africa with no government and no refuge, and the world did not understand why. Nor did we. Who were our enemies, and against whom were we fighting? Ourselves? It made no sense. My youthful mind could not comprehend why this was happening, but as I grew older and matured, I recognized there was more to the story.

Chapter Two

THE DECISION TO LEAVE

Factors leading to immigration

The desperation to escape the unrelenting violence pushed my family to make the heart-wrenching decision to leave our homeland behind. War, a relentless force of destruction, shattered our dreams and plunged us into a life of constant fear. The decision to immigrate to a refugee camp in Kenya became a beacon of hope in a sea of despair, promising the possibility of a future untouched by violence. This time, it was my aunt, her eight children, my mom, my siblings, and myself; there were twelve children. We had to travel behind cars and at night to avoid being caught at checkpoints. However, we faced a lack of resources and infrastructure, not to mention limited access to essential resources like water, food, and healthcare. The basic infrastructure that could prompt individuals to migrate to countries with better provision of these necessities felt out of reach for many. What we went through was discrimination at its core.

If we did not have the correct paperwork or refugee status, we would be subjected to mandatory jail sentences unless our family had the means to pay corrupt political officials. These officials functioned as gatekeepers to our freedom. It was excruciating—just the mere thought that your life was in the hands of someone who did not care whether you lived or not unless there was money on the table. That realization was hard to digest, mainly when those of your blood carried out such abusive breaches of power. Blood that they proudly displayed as so-called pride and revenge in honor of their respective tribe. At this point, it was akin to Nazi behavior.

CHALLENGES FACED

Leaving our homeland was painful, marked by emotional struggles and tearful farewells. At seventeen, I was chosen as the only family member to embark on a new journey. It felt like I was carrying the world's weight on my young shoulders. It symbolized my family's sacrifices, leaving behind loved ones and the remnants of the life we once knew. The hope for a better future was bittersweet, marred by the bitter taste of loss. For a young girl like me, with no experience outside my borders, aside from the abuse endured at boarding school, my world and my mind were constantly at war, not just my country. My internal conflict was that I loved my family dearly, but the environment I was subjected to felt like a never-ending roller-coaster of threats to my safety. This posed a dilemma. I felt safe in the arms of my family, but the thought of embarking on this uncertain journey was the moment that would continue to define my life—fight or die, persevere or perish; those were my options.

Chapter Three

THE VOYAGE

The Journey to the New Country

My journey to America was filled with uncertainty. Sponsored through a program, I found myself on a path to a new land, not knowing where it would lead.

Embarking on this journey meant leaving everything I once knew behind. I was in a foreign land, couldn't speak a foreign language, struggled to eat the new food, and couldn't wrap my head around the foreign culture. I was terrified and homesick. And felt incredibly out of my element. Immigrating was a sensory overload for me. I was overwhelmed by the difference in livelihood. The fear of the unknown gripped me, intensified by the isolation of leaving my family behind, their faces etched in my memory.

My aunt and my mother decided to send me to America since I was the youngest and I had a passion for education. They all hoped I would make a difference for myself and support our family. However, they had different plans in mind, like promising my hand in marriage to a man who lived in America.

Arrival and Immigration:

I arrived in the USA via car from Mexico. It was a long, arduous journey that took a lot out of me mentally. Coming to the checkpoint to enter the US felt surreal. And meeting my paternal aunt on the other side of the border was relieving. Knowing a familiar face helped soothe the nerves that were racking my brain. We then went deeper into American territory by a Greyhound bus and onto California. California looked much like Somalia because it was dry and desert-like. I genuinely believed at that moment that the entire world was like that. However, I was soon proven wrong as we went into Seattle, and all I remember for that was lush greenery on hilly surfaces. It was a new environment. I was enamored and continued to keep watching and learning what my new normal was to be. Interestingly, I wasn't dressed for that environment, wearing a blue summer dress, sandals, and a matching scarf; all I was thinking about was the urge to protect myself against the cold, for I wasn't used to the cold rainy weather Seattle presents.

Upon arrival in the new government, you will go through immigration and customs procedures. You have to show your passport, visa, and any supporting documents as required. Be prepared for potential questioning and ensure you have all the necessary paperwork readily accessible. My heart was beating. Did I have everything? My seventeen-year-old brain ran wild. What if I missed something and I was reprimanded and thrown in jail, never to see my family again?

That was the scariest thought because, to me, that was what I knew back home. Isolation was my worst fear. "Is this place as safe as they claimed?" I wondered. My distrust of the system began to show as my anxiety flared up. But I continued to think positive thoughts and keep myself calm—that was a matter of survival for me, an instinct I could not shed. Looking back at that moment, I felt genuinely resilient. Keeping my mother and siblings strong in my heart motivated me to keep pushing forward, and so I did.

I breathed deeply, saying, "One foot at a time—just one foot in front of the other." I was disciplined and knew that I could at least trust myself if I could not trust others. I glanced down at my little, ratted-up bag, filled with heaps of paperwork stored away for me in a translucent plastic bag—those papers and documents were necessary, and I knew this very well. Keeping calm, holding my anxiety deep inside, I told myself to breathe. With every slow inhalation and exhalation, I took out each required document individually, handing them over to officials with the steadiest hand I could muster. They accepted all the paperwork and proceeded to process my immigration without giving me a second look or saying a word to a child who could not speak a lick of English. In retrospect, they knew exactly what I had been through, and it did not make sense to question a child of war—this, I appreciated.

Settling In

Once you arrive, it is time to start fitting into my new country. I had to establish a new routine, a new way of life. This involved finding employment, enrolling in educational programs, or pursuing other personal goals. My goal here was to take advantage of the opportunities available in my new country and seek support from local resources and networks. The opportunities afforded by my new government were not lost on me. I wanted and needed my family to join me in this new, scary world that consisted of unfamiliar faces and a new way of life that I was still getting used to.

I was not part of the program anymore. I was trying to learn English and work together on my associate degree, and that's how I thought: if I can stand up for myself, keep going to the library, and keep studying, I can achieve my dream one day.

My environment was a melting pot of diversity; I was alone, and everything I knew was gone. Now, I just had to navigate these treacherous waters, which would be challenging. I needed to assimilate quickly, and there was no time to waste, but luckily, my unique journey up until then had prepared me to do just that.

Chapter Four

CHALLENGES DURING THE JOURNEY

Every moment of the journey was fraught with desperation and fear. The unfamiliarity of my destination, coupled with being in the presence of a stranger as my companion to an underage girl like me, added another layer of trust that I had not accounted for but needed to have faith in. The constant uncertainty of what lay ahead haunted my thoughts. Leaving my family behind intensified my pain, making each step a struggle against despair and isolation. But I continued to rely on my instincts, values, and undying belief in God, trusting He would see me through. I had faith—the type of faith that gives you hope and light at the end of the tunnel. So, I kept my feet steady and placed one foot in front of the other, one step at a time.

Cultural Differences

The United States is culturally diverse, and travelers may encounter cultural differences they need to navigate. Customs, social norms, and etiquette can vary across different regions and communities within the country. Being open-minded, respectful, and aware of cultural sensitivities is essential. This is what I had to learn fast, but I was ready. I was ready for new beginnings, finally prepared to encounter friendly faces and a new life that would change my perspective on this scary world. I always hoped to be in the company of good people who had my best interests in mind, away from the security of my aunt. I expected this time to be different.

Now, I was seventeen years old and had no parents. While it's expected to lean on your culture and learn from friends, I initially didn't do so. Perhaps I believed everything could be acquired without legal channels, avoiding cultural shock. However, being mindful of your actions and approach is essential. Being a young Muslim girl in a whole different world was scary on its own, but having to face that world alone was even more terrifying.

Chapter Five

FIRST IMPRESSIONS IN THE NEW COUNTRY

Arriving in California, I was torn between relief and profound sadness. Reuniting with my aunt provided a bittersweet familiarity, her features mirroring those of my departed father. The encounter stirred a whirlwind of emotions, blending relief with the stark reality of my isolation in this foreign country. As I settled in, I confronted the overwhelming grief and loneliness that had become my constant companions as I tried to assimilate—a poignant reminder of the sacrifices my family had made for the promise of a better life. However, my family had another agenda in mind: to marry me off to my first cousin, who was 35 years older than me. Because arranged marriages were a regular part of my culture, I had to oblige and obey their request for this structured and manufactured union. The marriage was solidified in December 2000 with a small gathering at my paternal aunt's house. The group, which was meant to be a wedding, amounted to 30 people in total. In our culture, we are used to weddings of over 300 people. I considered this insulting and demeaning of my values, which kick-started the marriage as unappealing. I had no choice in my dress, hairstyle, or makeup. I was put into a traditional Somali wedding dress, probably the night's highlight. I wasn't even allowed to be a part of the planning. Considering I was in a foreign land, there were barely any familiar faces at my wedding and zero friends as I'd left everything behind. I was isolated even before my marriage and into it.

Considering I was a teenager without any experience in marriage, I expected a fairytale husband, someone who would collaborate with me and with whom I could entrust my life, good and bad. I presumed I would marry a man worth marrying. Instead, I got a brute for a husband. He showed me what kind of man I did not want. My husband did not show me love. It turned out I was not able to love him. And things escalated further, and I soon became pregnant with my first child. My husband used tough love on me to make matters more difficult to fit into a new country and ensure I accessed the necessary resources and organized the proper paperwork. Like a green card to stay in the USA, just as he controlled how I was treated and how I slept.

I used to sneak out to the library between 10 in the morning and 1:30 PM because that's when my husband returned from work. Since he was the only one working, so I had to ensure he had food on the table. Otherwise, I would get yelled at because he said, "My wife is supposed to do that." At that point, the world around me seemed pointless. Furthermore, I realized there was no reason to blame someone else for what I was going through. I had to change my life for my child. This was bigger than me. I had another mouth to feed, but more importantly, I knew in my heart that this child would now depend on me for the rest of my life, and there was no way I was about to fail them—not when I was so close to becoming the woman my family relied on me to be. He worked, so I followed his rules.

Responsible and obedient in paving the way for the next generation of the tribe by taking care of our family and all their needs – this was always my mission, but a mission I constantly questioned.

So, I decided to stand up for myself and figured out how to live my life on my terms. Shows like Law and Order and libraries took an interest in my life, including my cousin pushing to control my life. Gradually, I became confident that I would never let anyone dictate my actions or life. One of those days, I called my cousin, whom I trusted on my mother's side of the family, for guidance. This vulnerability allowed our friendship to flourish, transforming us from cousins to best friends. He helped me understand our ingrained Somali culture, including all the nuances that I had refused to acknowledge but needed to come to terms with and accept. Our Somali culture was intricate, with expectations placed on people, tribal alliances, and condemned behaviors—I learned all of it. It enlightened me, as my cousin equipped me with the knowledge and armor to withstand the naysayers and backward-thinking individuals. To beat them at their own game, I needed to be wiser, wittier, and better at playing their manipulative tactics to maintain control. No one was ever going to control my undying spirit, especially those rancid thoughts that tore my beautiful country apart in the first place. My confidence solidified; I was no longer just a child of war but a warrior.

My trusted cousin began to call me every day to check on me, listen to my thoughts and experiences, and continue to instill hope in the face of adversity. He was my rock, consistently reiterating and validating my strength and blessings, most importantly, the benefits God entrusted me with—my beautiful daughter, who would look up to me. That was the fuel I needed to keep going and continue to pursue my purpose. If not for my own sake, I was determined to ensure my daughter had a suitable role model to show her what she was also capable of— but I knew I had to set that example myself. This became my new mission.

I became determined to take these opportunities in this new country and try to make something out of them.

for and support me and my children no matter what. That same year, I became pregnant with my fifth child. Nine months after giving birth, I went back to school. Over the next eight years, I got pregnant three more times. He helped me get my paperwork in order and assisted me in obtaining my citizenship. Now, nothing could stop me from going to school and getting my degree. He and I worked together to achieve the American Dream. Without him, I do not know what I would have done.

Navigating the New World

Navigating the Legal System: Understanding and navigating the legal system of a new country can be challenging. This includes obtaining necessary visas, understanding immigration processes, and accessing essential services such as healthcare and education.

Adapting to the Unfamiliar

Lesson one - Dress Appropriately: Pay attention to the local dress code and respectfully align with the new land's cultural norms. It shows that you are aware and respectful of the local customs.

Lesson number two - Be Punctual: Arrive on time for appointments, meetings, or social gatherings. Punctuality is often valued in many cultures and demonstrates your respect for other people's time.

Lesson Number Three - Show Respect: Be respectful towards the local culture, traditions, and customs. Observe and follow the social etiquette of the new land, such as greetings, gestures, and proper manners. Showing respect helps to establish positive connections with the locals.

Lesson number four - Be Open and Friendly: Approach new people with a smile and a friendly attitude. Be open to meeting unique individuals, engaging in small talk, and showing genuine interest in their culture and experiences. This can help create a welcoming and positive impression.

Lesson number five - Listen and Observe: Take the time to listen when conversing with others actively. Show interest in their stories, opinions, and perspectives. Additionally, observe and learn from the behavior and social cues of the locals to better understand the cultural dynamics.

Lesson number six - Be Mindful of Body Language: Non-verbal communication plays a significant role in making a first impression. Be aware of your body language, maintain eye contact, and use appropriate gestures acceptable in the new land.

Lesson number seven - Learn Basic Phrases: If the local language differs from your own, learn a few basic phrases to demonstrate your willingness to engage and communicate with the locals. Simple greetings, expressions of gratitude, and everyday words can go a long way in making a positive impression.

Lesson number eight - Avoid Stereotypes and Prejudices: Be conscious of any stereotypes or biases you may hold and avoid making assumptions about the new land or its people. Embrace diversity and approach others with an open mind.

Lesson nine - Be Patient and Understanding: Adapting to a new land takes time, and cultural differences or misunderstandings may occur. Be patient, understanding, and willing to learn from your experiences.

Lesson number ten – Be Authentic to yourself and your values as a whole: This is the most important lesson of them all. Never lose yourself in the chaos of this world; take all that you have learned and the values you align yourself with, stay true to your purpose, and uplift others to set an example. This is the lesson I hold dear. This is the lesson that saved my life.

The difficulty of being exposed to an unfamiliar environment from a familiar one is a remarkable experience. The discomfort of being thrust into a foreign world, trying to make sense of everything, and adapting to new surroundings is an overwhelming experience and journey. The fear and overthinking accompanying this transition create a profound sense of vulnerability.

The environment

Discrimination and Prejudice: Immigrants faced with discrimination, prejudice, or xenophobia in their new country were the latest game to navigate for those displaced by war or famine. They may encounter biases based on nationality, ethnicity, religion, or immigration status. Discrimination can affect their opportunities for employment, housing, education, and social inclusion.

Also, Keep an open Mind: Embrace new experiences and be open to learning and understanding the unfamiliar. Approach differences with curiosity rather than judgment and be willing to step outside your comfort zone. Connect the community instead of dividing it.

Learn about the Culture: Take the time to learn about the local culture, customs, and traditions. Read books, watch documentaries, or attend cultural events to better understand the people and their way of life. Engaging in artistic activities can also help you meet new people and make connections.

Learn the Language: If the new land has a different language, learning the local language can enhance your ability to adapt and integrate. Enroll in language classes, practice with language exchange partners, or use language learning apps to improve your language skills. Communicating with locals in their language can open doors to new opportunities and connections and build countless bridges within the contemporary community.

Build a Support Network: Seek opportunities to meet new people and build a dedicated support network. Join social or community groups, attend local events, or engage in activities that align with your interests. This can help you make friends, find support, and feel more connected to the new surroundings.

Stay Patient and Resilient: Adapting to the unfamiliar takes time, and it is essential to be patient with myself.

Accept that there may be challenges along the way and that it is okay to make mistakes. Constantly forgive me. Develop resilience by maintaining a positive mindset, focusing on growth opportunities, and learning that comes with the unfamiliar. You will become a stronger person because of it.

Chapter Six

STRUGGLES IN THE NEW LAND

Acceptance became a monumental hurdle. People, inherently wary of the unknown, kept their distance, viewing me as an alien figure—I was foreign not only in my origin but also in my traditions, appearance, culture, and beliefs. This alienation fostered profound feelings of isolation, leaving me without the much-needed support and sense of community for which I was so desperately longing. The mental toll of this isolation was staggering, but I continued to keep my head above water.

Employment and security became pressing concerns. Questions like, "What is my function in this society?" loomed. Navigating the workforce meant connecting with people vastly different from myself, a challenge that demanded breaking barriers of prejudice and bias. Establishing relationships and camaraderie required entering a space of open-mindedness and vulnerability and realizing that people were far more diverse than I had ever imagined.

The journey through this unfamiliar terrain was geographical and deeply psychological. It demanded resilience in the face of isolation and the courage to seek acceptance and understanding in a world that initially seemed resistant to embracing the foreign and the unfamiliar. This was the chess game I was now playing. However, with each passing year, my inner strength and the armor that my cousin/best friend equipped me with allowed me to have the courage to step into this world and take it on headfirst, like a gladiator in an arena. I finally understood the rules, but I also knew that women who followed the rules rarely made history. So, I was determined to make sure that, regardless of the outcome, I would make my mark by providing an impact and being a robust role model for my family and community.

Cultural adjustment: Immigrants may experience culture shock when encountering different social norms, customs, values, and traditions. Adapting to a new culture can take time and effort, and individuals may need to learn new social behaviors, etiquette, and cultural expectations.

I didn't know what to expect when I started this journey, but I was incredibly shocked at the difference between what I was used to and what was to be my new norm.

The diversity in America was very much missing

from where I came from. The different religions were a complete eye-opener and lifestyle shock for me.

Living alongside people of different races and sexualities was an entirely foreign concept to me that had me thinking that everything I ever knew was because of the small bubble I lived in. Learning that our world was incredibly diverse and inclusive was a lesson I was delighted to discover.

Homesickness: Missing one's home country, family, and friends is a common experience when moving to a new land. Adjusting to an unfamiliar environment and developing a sense of belonging can take time.

All the factors mentioned above helped me navigate this unique world and the ins and outs associated with being a displaced individual, a struggle that many of us go through daily. The constant threat to my individuality and livelihood is not lost on me. As a warrior for human connection and resilience, my newfound mission is to help those navigating the same challenges I faced when I first entered this new country. This is something I am genuinely enthusiastic about to my core. I acknowledge that I was one of the few lucky ones to make it out alive, but my work is not done. The blessings were indeed real. As a mother of not just one but eight children, my desire to be a role model has only compounded my drive to balance it all and lead by example.

The lesson here is to equip myself with knowledge, make space in this world to heal others, and have their voices heard—a sentiment I live by and aspire to inspire in others as a beacon of light. This has led me to continue my education, receive my associate degree, and work on my bachelor's in psychology to fulfill this purpose I wholeheartedly believe in. This belief in myself is my redeeming quality. By becoming a psychologist one day, I hope to make a difference in at least one life, creating a ripple effect of community building that lasts a lifetime. My mission is set, and the wheels are in motion because there is no such thing as impossible—the word itself provides me solace in that it combines "I'm possible."

Epilogue

I have been waiting to become a US citizen for 22 years. I finally became one in July last year. I became a United States citizen. It also has taken me 22 years to maintain an associate degree in psychology. Today, I graduated top of my class with eight children.

As regards my cousin, my best friend… He tragically passed away in a truck accident in Arizona on February 26. We had dinner together that Saturday and discussed plans to open a business. He promised to return the following weekend, but that never happened.

I became increasingly worried when he didn't answer my weekly calls. It was only when I saw the news about two men dying in a trucking accident that I realized the severity of the situation. Seeing his picture shook me to the core; I felt like I was losing my own life, struggling to breathe and move.

I immediately contacted the police and booked the

soonest flight to Arizona, not even considering the distance. The normally eight-hour flight turned into a two-day journey as I was desperate for answers. Arriving in Arizona, I met the family of the other man involved in the accident. Knowing they were best friends for five years devastated me further; they were inseparable.

On Friday evening, I saw my cousin's remains; all I could identify were his teeth. I recall the doctor mentioning the need for a DNA sample for our grandma. Taking the DNA felt like someone was holding a knife to my throat amidst panic and tears, surrounded by many people.

I spent five days there, feeling like an eternity. Upon returning to Columbus, I looked at my children and realized I needed to gather myself for them. My mind was far from school or studies. It was then that I sought help from a school psychologist to piece my life back together. Through their guidance, I found ways to cope, even amidst the pain and confusion. It's been a challenging journey, but seeking help has been my anchor in rebuilding my life.

BE CONTINUED.

Notes

Arranged marriage – about Somali people – back in the day, she was promised to someone else, but the family disapproved due to tribal conflict. Tribes are more critical to your identity than the pursuit of your happiness… which is why the arranged marriage arose so that we could stick to the same tribe.

Even though I have been through it all, I never gave up on school.